C000058704

POOPING PETS

PETS

THE DOG EDITION

CHARLIE ELLIS

summersdale

POOPING PETS: THE DOG EDITION

An Hachette UK Company
www.hachette.co.uk

Summersdale Publishers Ltd
Part of Octopus Publishing Group Limited
Carmelite House
50 Victoria Embankment
LONDON
EC4Y 0DZ
UK

www.summersdale.com

Printed and bound in China

ISBN: 978-1-80007-641-9

Substantial discounts on bulk quantities of Summersdale books are available to corporations, professional associations and other organizations. For details contact general enquiries: telephone: +44 (0) 1243 771107 or email: enquiries@summersdale.com.

To.................................

From.............................

No buried treasure here, I'm afraid. Just last night's dinner.

You just take up a position like so, release the ol' sphincter, and the poop slides right out.

Beep-beep! I'm backing up this dump truck and dropping a heavy load of topsoil.

Hehehe, so much for "no fouling"!

I don't care that you've just laid these tiles. I've just laid these cables.

I'm trying, but this one's stuck halfway out! Help a doggo out, would you, and pull?

Can't hang with the
big dogs until I learn
to poop like one.

Looks like those kids are collecting pebbles. Maybe I can help them out with some pebbles of my own.

We're gonna need
a bigger poop mat.

I can fire these out
like rockets. Take cover!

I knew wolfing
down that curry
was a bad idea.

Did you say your lovely lawn needs some fresh fertilizer?

Oh no, it's the puparazzi!
Of all the moments
to be caught!

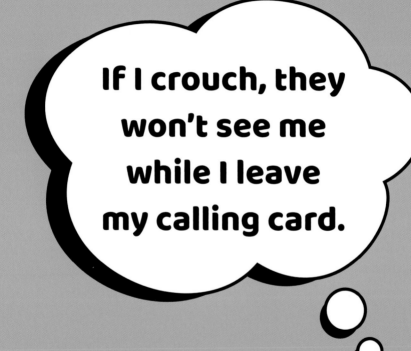

Bears aren't the only creatures that lay one out in the woods.

Can you make yourself useful and come and wipe me?

I hate to say it, but
I might need another
shampoo when I'm done
with this — it's gonna
be a messy one!

Pick up my poop, human!
I have things to do!

Nugs! Hot, fresh dog nugs! Come and get 'em!

If you rush me
again, I'll save a few
of these for your
slippers, Jeffrey.

Yeah that's right,
stare deep into
my eyes.

I'm a Chocolate Lab: come see my chocolate factory in production mode!

Those humans are on to something — it is easier to poop in a seated position!

Why do you insist on collecting all of it? You should get a normal hobby.

Just adding a log
to these branches.

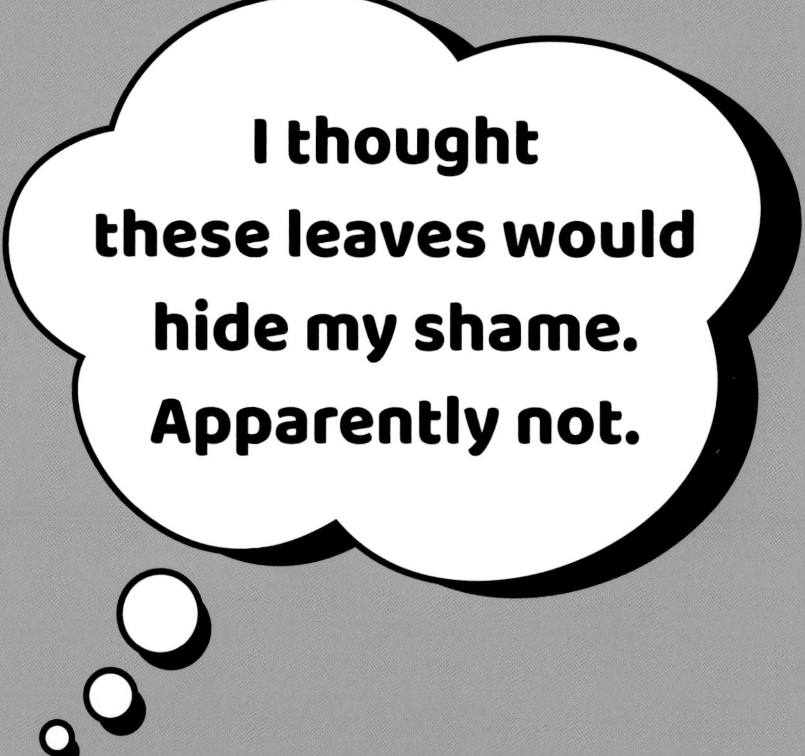
I thought these leaves would hide my shame. Apparently not.

Can we go home now? 'Cause I really need to poop.

I thought it was just
a fart — I thought
it was safe!

Ocean, hear my bottom's
call and swallow up
my turdy tribute with
your salty brine!

It's not about the size of the dog — it's about the size of the poop.

I'm trying to curl one out
to match my little tail!

Image credits

Have you enjoyed this book? If so, find us on Facebook at **Summersdale Publishers**, on Twitter at **@Summersdale** and on Instagram at **@summersdalebooks** and get in touch. We'd love to hear from you!

www.summersdale.com